Visions of SAINT LUCIA

Rodney Bay Marina in the waning light

Introduction

Saint Lucia

Famed for its mystical Pitons, two volcanic peaks that rise dramatically out of the ocean and stand sentinel over the island, Saint Lucia is a geographically and culturally diverse nation of 238 square miles, a vital link in the archipelago that arcs the expansive Caribbean Sea.

The Land

The Piton landmarks have graced the covers of magazines the world over, lending Saint Lucia a visibility and recognition that distinguishes the small Windward Island from its sister nations. But the Pitons are just the beginning of Saint Lucia's marvels. The island is possessed of such varied and dramatic landscape as to keep the observer in constant awe. The agitated Atlantic crashes against the arid and rugged terrain of the east, characterised by sparse, wind beaten succulents and brush. From the coast the land rises, turning a deep rainforest palette of greens towards its interior before undulating gently into coconut palm fringed coves and bays along the west coast.

The People

Saint Lucia is however as much an historical phenomenon as a geographic wonder. The island has been coveted as one of the most sought-after addresses in the world, a distinction established as early as pre-Colombian times when Amerindians inhabited the island. Evidence of their predilection is found in the petroglyphs they left behind, and findings during a recent discovery of an important ceremonial burial site suggest it was a symbolic centre for the Windward Islands. Its strategic and emblematic importance has persisted throughout European contact, and the result is a legacy that has bestowed the culture with the unique texture and colour that characterises it today.

It was Dutch sailors who constituted the first encounter of the west with the ruggedly beautiful island in 1600 but no attempt at settlement was made before 1605 when shipwrecked English sailors aboard the Olive Branch destined for Guyana decided to make a go of things. Their attempts were doomed, the result of disease and conflict with the Carib population, and though there were several fits and starts in the subsequent years, it wasn't until a century later that a serious colonising effort was able to establish itself. When that happened the island was catapulted into the limelight as the scene of early imperial struggles between the European powers which so coveted the island that it was soon given the moniker Helen of the West.

The conflict was not over the treasures of spices and minerals such as were yielded by Central and South America. Saint Lucia was valued as much for its strategic location as for its production of sugar, and its by-product rum.

The island falls midway down the archipelago, making it an ideal launching point for the imperial navies that defended the French and English territories respectively. The same held for pirates like the notorious Jambe de Bois who stashed his booty at Pigeon Island and fended off

Aerial view of Marigot

The National Colours of St. Lucia

interlopers to the birth of many a legend. The island became a battleground between European interests who had a stake in the lucrative sugar industry which would later become the mainstay of the fledgling national economy. The labour intensive sugar production demanded more labour than could be supplied by the indigenous populations and slave labour from Africa was introduced. The African population would soon form the major demographic base of the islands. Indentured labour and the small European population that remained after emancipation would contribute to the melting pot culture that the island is now known for.

That unique experience has yielded two Nobel laureates, the Honourable Derek Walcott for Literature, and Sir Arthur Lewis for Economics and Saint Lucia has continued to be a source of cultural innovation which has long inspired and intrigued the rest of the Caribbean.

The Light

The photographer or artist is never bored in Saint Lucia, opportunity emerges in every bend in the winding road that skirts the coast, and with every change of light, each scene is washed anew. The diversity of influences on the island's early development meant that the emerging nation of Saint Lucia, when it was it first flew its flag in the blustery trade winds of February in 1979, was to draw together these disparate influences under one nation, one ideal – a country forged from a series of conflicts to represent the ultimate synthesis, as so much of the Caribbean represents, of indigenous, European and African. The influences of the French and English who played out a century-long conflict over the island, persist in the language and religion, and the education and judicial systems respectively. This fusion is given expression in the faces of the people, the colour of its folkloric practices, the fresh variety of its agricultural bounty, and most notably in the language of Kwéyòl: a way of life as well as a mode of expression and one that pays homage to the idea that out of many influences, one nation is forged.

The Way

Fishing and agricultural communities have formed the basis of the island's development which has quickly extended in its short history into the manufacturing and tertiary sectors. The community based society plays an integral part in the character and appeal to tourism which has in latter years become the island's most important industry. That has been further facilitated not only by Saint Lucia's natural beauty, year-round clement conditions, and easygoing lifestyle, but also by a developing infrastructure and a concerted strategy of investment-friendly policies.

The landscape of Saint Lucia has shifted over the years but our legacy dances lightly among us – though the sprawling valleys, all the more impressive because of the steep mountain ridges which flirt its boundaries, and over the diverse people and their celebratory approach to life centred around food and drink, festival, tradition and warmth and hospitality.

Contents

Aerial view of Castries Harbour

The coast is a central part of St Lucian life

SAILING INTO PARADISE...THE LUSH GREEN LANDSCAPES AND CRYSTAL-CLEAR WATERS OF THE COASTLINE, ATTRACT MANY VISITORS EACH YEAR

Downtown Soufriere, once the island's capital

● 'The Aftermath', sculpture by Ricky George - ECFH Group Centre, Castries

St. Joseph the Worker Catholic Church in the glow of evening mass, Gros Islet

EVIDENCE OF THE COLONIAL STRUGGLE BETWEEN THE BRITISH AND FRENCH PERSISTS IN THE SURVIVING BRICK WORK OF THEIR MILITARY COMPLEXES, VIGIE

Port of Call - the marina and Castries Harbour by night

THE GOVERNMENT BUILDINGS AT THE WATERFRONT, CASTRIES

The traditional fishing community of Anse La Raye

Rodney Bay Marina, among the Caribbean's most desirable marinas, Gros Islet

A panoramic view from Moule a Chique

Arial view of Pointe Seraphine

Carnival Destiny

A Breathtaking vantage of the island's world-famous Pitons

All signs point to Rodney Bay, the island's recreation and tourism centre, Gros Islet

IREE

A MODEST COUNTRY-SIDE HOUSE, BIG ON SCENERY

THE ICONIC BELL TOWER OF THE CATHEDRAL OF THE IMMACULATE CONCEPTION, CASTRIES

RAYS OF NATURAL LIGHT INSPIRE THE FAITHFUL - CATHEDRAL OF THE IMMACULATE CONCEPTION

SOUFRIERE'S CHURCH OF THE ASSUMPTION OF THE BLESSED LADY

Church of the Nativity of the Blessed Virgin at Anse La Raye

A portal to the island's past, Fort Rodney, Pigeon Island

Remote and less accessible than the Caribbean Sea, the Atlantic coast is a sweep of unspoiled beauty

Where sky and sea meet is promise, hope and new beginnings

St Lucia's intrigue and mystery extends from sea to sky

A BEACHCOMBER'S REWARD

DRAMATIC ROCK FORMATIONS CHARACTERISE THE ISLAND'S EAST COAST, FOND D'OR, DENNERY

Coconut grove at dusk

At rest, the fishing boat belies the activity and excitement of the catch

FORT RODNEY PRESIDES OVER THE SANDALS IDYLL, PIGEON ISLAND

Coastline of Dramatic Beauty...

Horse Riding tour adventure

A SNORKELLER'S DREAM - THE SHALLOW REEFS OF THE CARIBBEAN COAST

View through coastal grove at Cas-en-bas Bay

● The iconic Pitons take on mythical proportions by moonlight, Soufriere

The Brig Unicorn in the shade of Petit Piton, Soufriere

A cooling reprieve for horse and rider at Cas-en-bas

The final descent into the town of Soufriere

Mending nets to secure the catch

An explosion of Bougainvillea frames Dennery's Fond D'or Bay

Gingerbread cottages peep from the hillside, Fond Doux Estate

Royal palms against a cloudless sky

● Vendors set up for the day's trade on Jeremie Street, Castries

A quiet day at Pigeon Island Bay

THE WHOLE VILLAGE COMES TOGETHER TO BRING IN THE CATCH, GROS ISLET

A REMOTE WEST COAST BAY

THE FLOATING VENDOR: BANANAS, COCONUTS, PAW PAW

● ONCE MILITARY BARRACKS, NOW HOME TO THE ST LUCIA NATIONAL TRUST, PIGEON ISLAND

A rainbow's benediction over the island's interior

The Colours of Carnival...

CARNIVAL IS ALL ABOUT LIFE AND EXPRESSION, NO MATTER HOW OLD

Kiddie's Carnival falls the weekend before the main street festivities and is a wonderful family affair

The young revellers parade across the main stage for the judging panel

In addition to assessing the design and symbolism of the costumes, judges look for expression and comportment of the young participants as a group

Bank of Saint
ARIB
ABLE
RNATIONA
VICE. BETTER NE

THE FOLLOWING WEEK, THE ADULT REVELLERS TAKE TO THE STREETS

FEATHERS, BEADS AND SEQUINS REIGN SUPREME

LIME

Contestants vie for King and Queen of the Band titles

Carnival
2009
Digicel

● BY THE SECOND DAY, SOME OF THE FEATHERS HAVE DROPPED AND REVELLERS CHIP MORE SLOWLY THOUGH NO LESS ENTHUSIASTICALLY DOWN THE ROAD

Carnival is about letting go, a sanctioned release from the confines of day to day society

A RIDING TOUR AMBLES ALONG THE CRESCENT BAY OF CAS-EN-BAS

Life On the Beach...

A HOLIDAY WEEKEND BRINGS BATHERS OUT IN NUMBERS

THOUGH ENJOYING A BRISK TOURISM TRADE, SOUFRIERE BAY MAINTAINS A TRANQUIL ATMOSPHERE

YAMAHA
J6-998

Beached fishing boats lie in dramatic scenery

Fishing from the shore, an activity the whole family can enjoy

The serene natural beauty of Calabash Cove

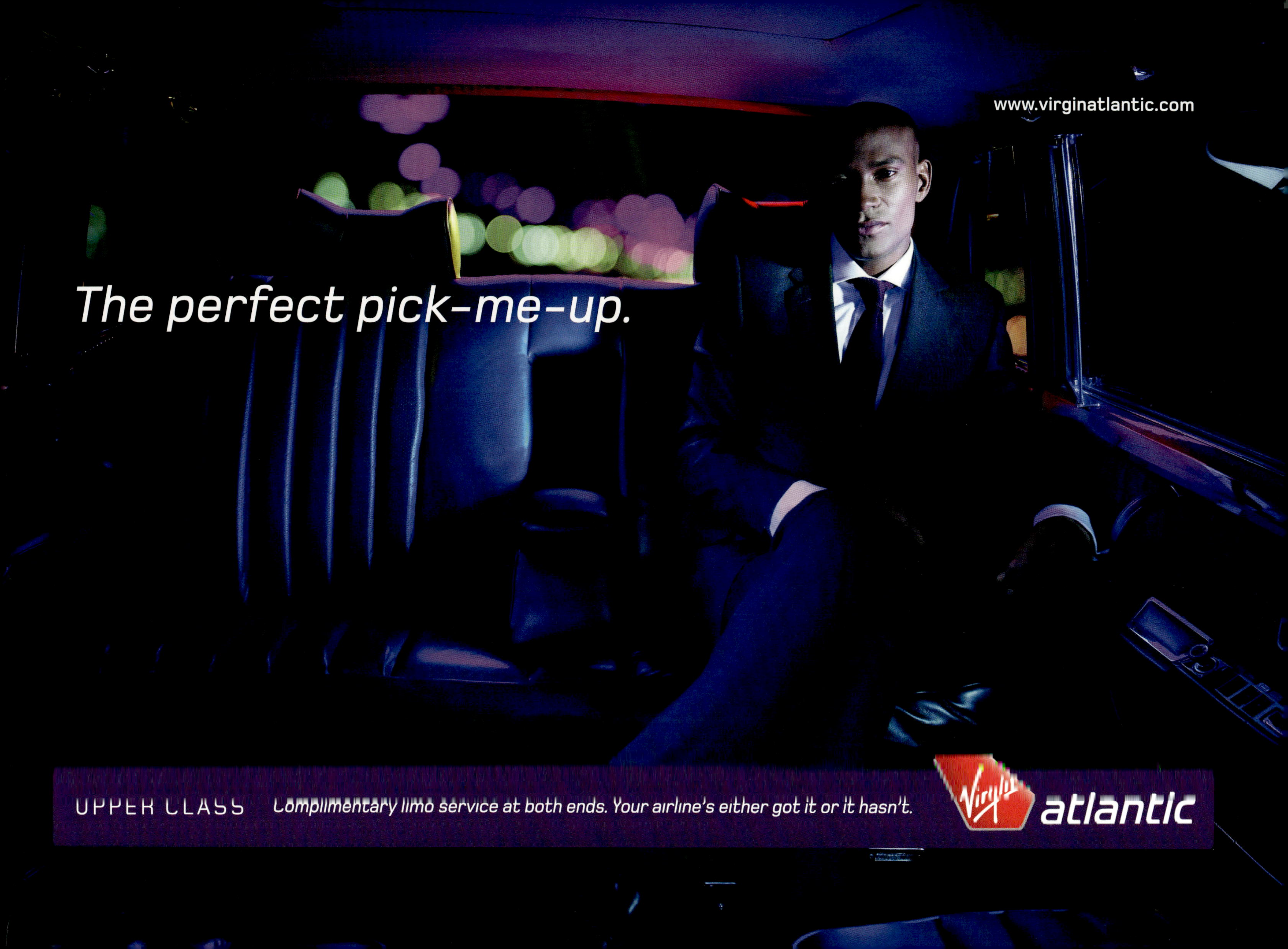
www.virginatlantic.com
The perfect pick-me-up.
UPPER CLASS
Complimentary limo service at both ends. Your airline's either got it or it hasn't.
Virgin atlantic

● Picture postcard scenes present themselves at every turn

Stunning seascapes are constant, it's the quality of the changing skies that brings variety

The Beach at East Winds Inn

One of the prettiest beaches in the Caribbean, Reduit Beach

Labrelotte Bay looks across to the Vigie Peninsular

A TRANQUIL BEACH IN THE FISHING VILLAGE OF LABORIE

The tranquil north end of Soufriere Bay

A Soufriere fishing community

Perhaps the most idyllic mooring on earth, Petit Piton Soufriere

● ROSES AMONG SPINDLY SEA URCHIN THORNS (BLACKBAR SOLDIER FISH)

Reef of Abundant Sea Life

Four-eyed Butterfly Fish

Purple and Yellow Tube Sponge

From left to right: Christmas Tree Worms on Brain Coral, Banded Coral Shrimp, Feather Duster Worm, Octopus peeking out from it's den, A Red Frog Fish

A diver cuddling a Sea Cucumber

Purple Vase Sponge

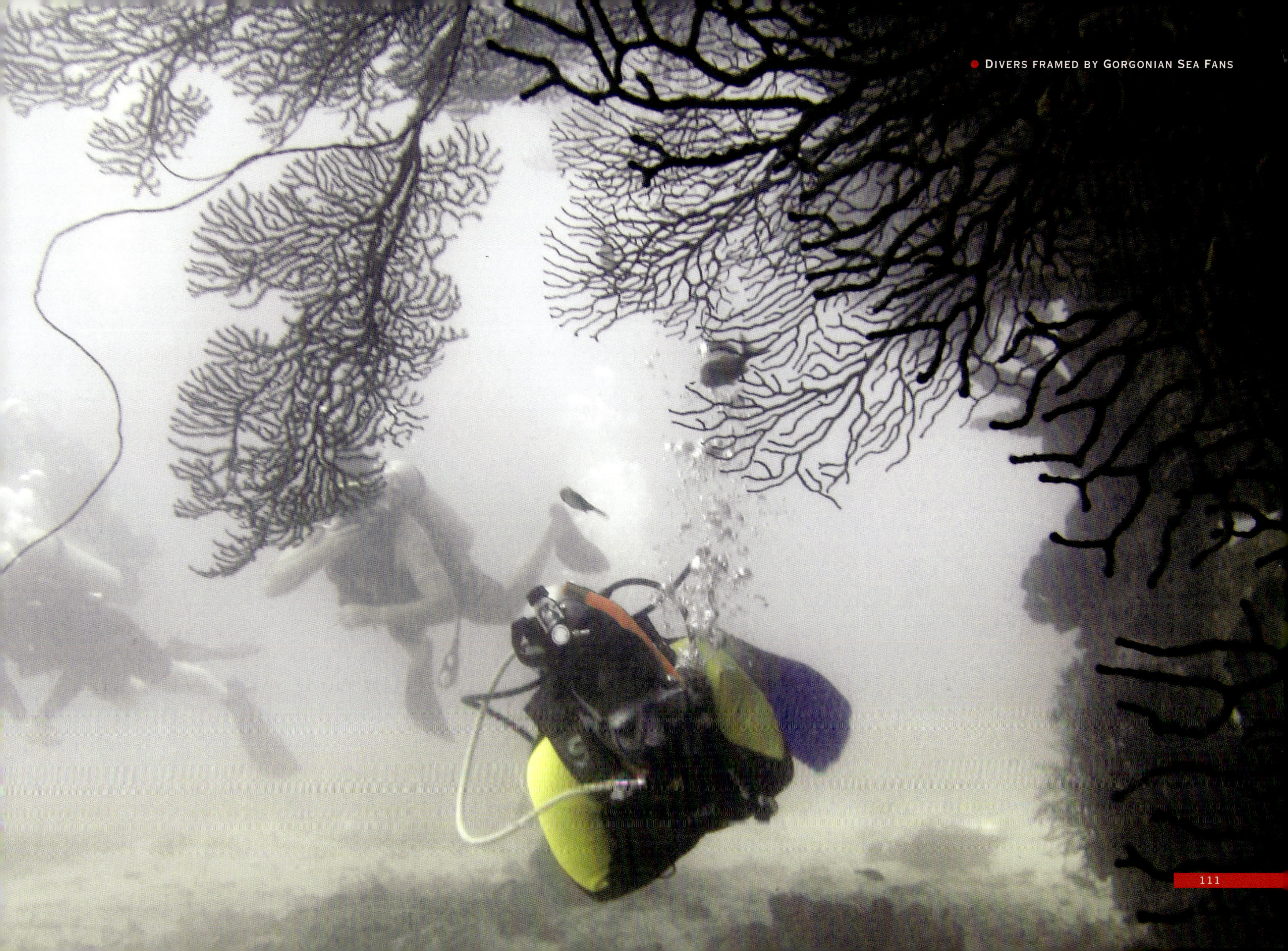

Divers framed by Gorgonian Sea Fans

● Divers watching a Barracuda

● Caribbean Reef Squid

● Section of Rosemund Trench reef showing divers, Barrel Sponges, Tube Sponges and Brain Coral

A Hawksbill Turtle

Hundreds of Yellow Gobies swimming amongst the Fire Coral

The impressive Flamingo Tounge Sea Snail

Diver looking through a section of the Lesleen M wreck

Juvenile Queen Angel Fish

Yellow Frog Fish

Hawksbill Turtle swims serenely past rockbed

Spotlight Parrot Fish

A diver's view of the Pitons

SANDALS DIVE BOAT AT PETIT PITON

LEFT TO RIGHT:

- [illegible]
- THE WRECK AT LESLEEN M (VIEW FROM THE BOW)
- [illegible]

The Vivid Colours of Saint Lucia

The hardy but colourful blossom of the canon ball tree

The Wax Rose

The vivid flower of the Flamboyant tree

THE MANY VARIETIES OF TROPICAL FLORA AND FRUIT

A Japanese bridge in a tropical garden

The hardy but beautiful pine cone Ginger Lily

THE DIAMOND FALLS, SOUFRIERE

Wild Saint Lucia...

Freshwater bathing holes are central to St Lucia recreational life

The River 'lime', a St Lucian institution

This colourful caterpillar will soon metamorphose into the large Hawk Moth

THE UBIQUITOUS WHITE EGRET ON ITS PERCH

Prickly virtue. These dried shrubs have medicinal properties and are also used in flower arrangements

The vibrant pink flowers of the Water Lily

A White Egret takes flight

A Cattle Egret with its distinctive orange mowhawk

THE VAST RAINFOREST RECLAIMS FALLOW LAND

THE ANTILLEAN CRESTED HUMMINGBIRD

THE MINERAL RICH WATERS OF THE WATERFALLS OF SOUFRIERE

St Lucia's interior is a network of mountain ridges that are largely preserved

A RIVER BATH REFRESHES AND REINVIGORATES

The boiling craters of the Sulphur Springs

Deceptively still, the watchful Sand Crab is lightning quick

Ideally located mid-way down the archipelago, St Lucia is a yacht haven

The love of Competition..

The sun sets on Rodney Bay Marina

Off to a great start, one of the island's many sailing regattas

All in a day's work, the racing boats head back to the docks, Rodney Bay

Competition is fierce on an island regatta

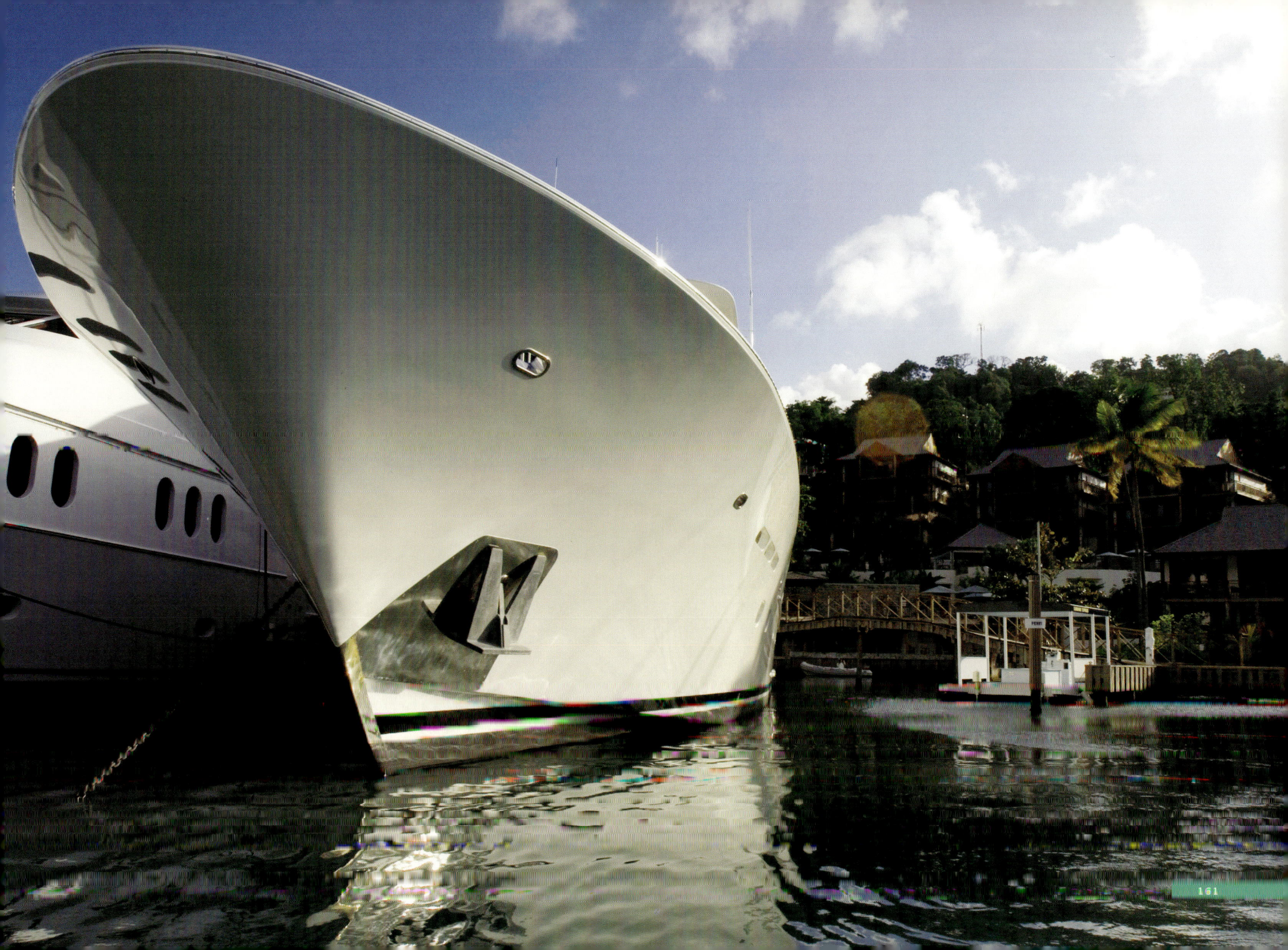

● St Lucia famously plays host to the Atlantic Rally for Cruisers (ARC)

The Atlantic connection – an ARC participant from Portugal

Immaculate greens, St Lucia Golf & Country Club

● ST LUCIA MOTOR CROSS PARTICIPANT SOARS HIGH

● DREAMS OF LARA AND SIR VIV ON A MAKESHIFT CRICKET PITCH, GRANDE RIVIERE

St Lucian youth practicing the universal language of football

Dame Marie Selipha Sesenne Descartes

The gentle folk of Saint Lucia

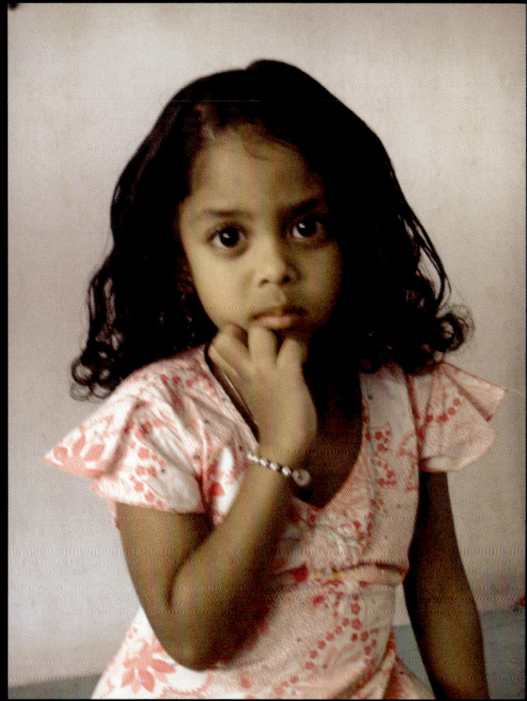

The true St Lucian landscape is its people

A VISION OF INFINITY - JADE MOUNTAIN, SOUFRIERE

Room with a Spectacular View...

Reflections of elegance at the Auberge Seraphine

THE PITONS FORM THE FOURTH WALL OF ROOMS AT THE CELEBRATED JADE MOUNTAN

A secluded retreat, the Smuggler's Nest is a favourite with honeymooners

The Rex St Lucian at Reduit Beach

Pool at the Auberge Seraphine

An endless horizon from the veranda of a Windjammer Landing Resort Villa

Memories of the Mediterranean - Windjammer Landing Resort

No two sunsets alike, the Caribbean dusk at Windjammer Landing

Day's end at Calabash Cove

A very private paradise, Calabash Cove

● An exclusive residential resort - The Landings

The inner harbour at Rock Resorts' The Landings

Balance, harmony and nature at Jade Mountain

Enjoy these well-appointed, two-bedroom villas situated in Trouya, with panoramic countryside and Caribbean views. There are two air-conditioned master bedrooms upstairs with en suite shower room. Each villa has queen size beds, soaking pool and patio with a view. On the lower level, there is a fully-equipped kitchen, dining area with television, DVD player and Hi-Fi system. There are laundry facilities with washer/dryer and iron. The villas accommodate up to six and housekeeping is available Monday through Friday.

FOR RESERVATIONS, CONTACT:
Travel Concepts, Inc.
Tel: 758-458-2243/4 or 758-451-0853
Email: tci@candw.lc
www.grandviewvillasstlucia.com

AFTER HOURS, CONTACT:
Tel: 758-484-9375 or
758-713-8881
Fax: 758-451-6092

Creole colonial - a picturesque villa at Fond Doux Holiday Plantation

A truly West Indian experience, from gingerbread eaves and mahogany beds, the drying cocoa – Fond Doux Holiday Plantation

Reprieve from the heat, poolside at Coco Palm Resort

Coco Palm Resorts - colonial charm with a modern twist

● Soufriere's charms, sea to sky

LADERA RESORT BOASTS SOME OF THE MOST SPECTACULAR SCENERY IN THE CARIBBEAN

Sandals
Sandals

A stretch of causeway joining the mainland to Pigeon Island National Park is home to Sandals Grande Resort

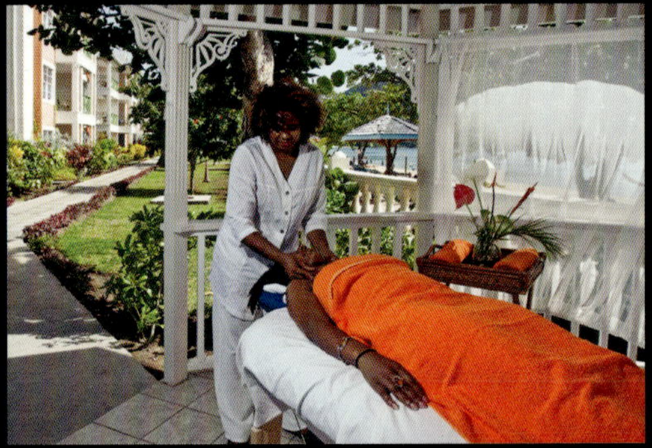

Poolside at Bay Gardens Beach resort, Rodney Bay

View from Calabash Cove - in the distance Castries and the historical Morne Fortune in a pre-dark glow

heaven
HEALTH SPA • CHAMPAGNE BAR
heaven...
a sanctuary of peace for mind, body & spirit
This state of the art spa and retreat takes you to sheer bliss. A journey that begins
herbal infusions continues with massage, facial, or body ritual that will leave you glowing. Heaven will create individual experiences of your choice.
Our unique environment provides a journey, uniting the bodies senses. Treatment
for choice & cherish yourself & loved ones. To find out more . . .
Call: 1 (758) 456 7500
COTTON BAY VILLAGE . PO BOX 2374 . ST LUCIA . WEST INDIES
Tel. +1 758 456 5700 . Fax. + 1 758 450 9518
Email: reservations@cottonbaystlucia.com . www.cottonbayvillage.com

For Reservations in one of our beautiful villas from the UK
Call. +44 (0)208 874 9900
In the USA & Canada
Call. +1 877 275 4975
CHILL OUT BY THE BEACH

A CANVAS WORTHY SCENE AT GROS ISLET

Awe-Inspiring Sunsets...

Royal Palms stand sentry as nightfall descends

A view of the distinctive peaks of Pigeon Island from Reduit Beach

The sun's rays over Tapion Point

A profile of Castries Harbour at sunset

Remnants of the jetty at La Toc Bay

● Crashing surf at Reduit Beach

Sunset casts everything in silhouette, Gros Islet pier

St Lucian youths stroll through the surf in the dying hours of daylight, Reduit Beach

River to sea at Vigie Beach

● Dusk at Reduit Beach

Stillness after sunset

● TROPICAL SILHOUETTE

The stroll back home in the last light of the day, Vigie Beach

● QUIET BEFORE THE STORM - BIG CHEF STEAKHOUSE BEFORE THE DINNER RUSH

Flavours of Saint Lucia...

NATURE'S PALETTE INSPIRES THE ISLAND'S ART

Ganter's Bay Marina from Jacque's Restaurant

Chef Orlando at Dashene Restaurant at Ladera serves up unique Caribbean cuisine. The view he says is complimentary

Fresh Caribbean bounty elevated to art

Come See the Beauty, Savour the Taste and Feel the Rhythm of St. Lucia on your own terms.

Greetings:

Since opening our doors in 2001 as a Travel and Destination Management Company, our business has grown and excelled by providing exceptional customer experiences. Travel Concepts reflects our intimate knowledge of the travel industry and an insistence on building lasting relationships with clients, as a core value of the company. Our years of experience allow us to effectively execute the following services:

- *Destination Management Services, Meetings and Incentives*
- *Airport Meet & Greet and Departure Services*
- *Airport & Seaport Transfers by Luxury Car, Coach and Helicopter*
- *Customized Sightseeing & Special Interest Tours, Sports Program Management*
- *Concierge Services, Villa Rentals, Adventure Experiences*
- *Educational programs with customized itineraries in any area of learning.*

Travel Concepts has a full service retail division providing support for the above services. Our strength is creativity and attention to detail. Our service is truly a labour of love!

Sincerely,

Jacqueline Austin, Managing Director

TRAVEL CONCEPTS INCORPORATED

Your exploration of the natural beauty and charm of the Island of St. Lucia can be made more worthwhile with Travel Concepts. Come and experience what sets us apart — our knowledge of the Island and our ability to use that knowledge to suit your specific needs. **www.travelconceptsstlucia.com**

Delivering Superior Services with Passion and Pride

SANS SOUCI OFFICE

#7 Maurice Mason Avenue

Tel: 758-458-2243/4 or 758-458-1853

Fax: 758-451-6892 | **Email:** tci@candw.lc

Caribbean Hotel & Tourism Association SLHTA site

Al fresco dining on the strip at Rodney Bay

THE COAL POT AT GANTERS BAY

Before the rush - cocktail hour at Auberge Seraphine

Earn your
SUN DOLLARS™
at Windjammer
Landing Resort
Up to 30% in
Incredible Credits!*
*SUN DOLLARS™ credits are good
for services, amenities and day tours.
Visit our website for full details.
Rising above a sea of resorts
Simple pleasures – simple beauty – simply the best resort in St. Lucia. It starts with a warm island welcome as you settle into your own private villa. Enjoy the breathtaking views from our gorgeous hillside setting and breathe in the lush tropical oasis that cascades down to the beachside. Dining destinations abound - each of our five restaurants features its own unique ambiance and delectable menu selections. Whatever your pleasure, Windjammer makes your visit unforgettable.
(877) 522-0722
(800) 958-7376
Windjammer®
LANDING
VILLA BEACH RESORT, ST. LUCIA
www.windjammer-landing.com
Experience the difference

Razmataz
Tandoori

Ku de Ta

RITUALS COFFEE
RITUALS COFFEE

REHAB REHAB REHAB REHAB
REHAB REHAB REHAB

Where there is Light,
there is Love.
Exclusively At
Di Diamonds International®
Pointe Seraphine & La Place Carenage Castries
Windjammer Landing Villa Beach Resort & Spa
Bay Walk Mall • Coconut Bay, Vieux Fort, St. Lucia
Crown of Light™
Irresistibly Brilliant™
www.crownoflight.com

H.E. the Governor General of St Lucia, Dame Pearlette Louisy

Famous Sons & Daughters of Saint Lucia...

Artist Llewellyn Xavier

LEVERN SPENCER

DARREN SAMMY

NADINE GEORGE

HOTELIERS WALTRUDE PATRICK AND BERTHIA PARLE

Saint Lucia Jazz Festival...

Luther Francois

Boo Hinkson

Jazz lovers soak up the atmosphere at Pigeon Island National Park

Kassav

Fate Sisters

Teddyson John

Natania

Khalid Barbara

George Duke

Estelle

Monty Dean

Beres Hammond

Ricardo Francois

SAINT LUCIA
JAZZ

GUY'S
CAR RENTAL

offers a fleet of well-maintained, current model vehicles to meet your every need - whether you are here on business or pleasure. Guy's Car Rental is strategically located in Castries. Choose Guy's Car Rentals during your stay in beautiful St. Lucia.

GUY'S

Pure Comfort

Attractive Rates

Current Models

24-Hour Hotline

Professional Service

Phone 758-451-7885 or 758-451-7147 • After Hours Phone: 758-450-6936
Fax: 758-453-2374 • Email info@guyscarrental.com • www.guyscarrental.com

Music lovers unite

TC Brown

Soca Monarch...

KAKAL

ESTEBAN

SUPERMAN

MANTIUS

JESSICA

TIAH MAN

PLATINUM

PRIVATE

RICKY T

WINTER

MINELLE

Global influences converge in the island's architecture

Famous visitors to our shores

● Sea Almond trees at sunset

The flower festivals of St Lucia

The happy couple at the Pink Plantation House

Government House, Morne Fortune

End of day at Auberge Seraphine